Jubilee
A Sacred Pause

A Scriptural Exploration of Rest

Rev. Dr. Loretta Faye Baker

BK Royston Publishing
bkroystonpublishing@gmail.com
www.bkroystonpublishing.com

Copyright © 2025 by Loretta F. Baker

All Rights Reserved. No part of this book may be reproduced, stored in a retrieval system, or transmitted by any means without the written permission of the author.

Cover and Layout: Elite Book Covers

ISBN: 978-1-967282-92-0

Unless otherwise indicated, all Scripture quotations are taken from the Holy Bible, New Living Translation, copyright © 1996, 2004, 2007 by Tyndale House Foundation. Used by permission of Tyndale House Publishers, Inc., Carol Stream, Illinois 60188. All rights reserved.

Printed in the United States of America

DEDICATION

To My Family

ACKNOWLEDGEMENTS

Special thanks to Denise for encouraging me every step of the way. Without your open spirit, this offering may not have manifested.

TABLE OF CONTENTS

Dedication		iii
Acknowledgements		iv
Introduction		vii
Today	Rest for the Soul	1
Week 1	Rest After the Rain	5
Week 2	Rest Beneath the Shade	9
Week 3	Resting in Sacred Spaces	13
Week 4	Rest in His Presence	17
Week 5	Reverence and Rest	21
Week 6	A Rhythm of Rest	25
Week 7	When the Land Rests Without Us	29
Week 8	Rest Along the Way	33
Week 9	Rest in the Promised Place	37
Week 10	Remember the Promise of Rest	41
Week 11	Helping Others Find Rest	45
Week 12	Rest on Every Side	49
Week 13	Rest Beyond Revenge	53
Week 14	Rest in the Rhythm of Grace	57
Week 15	Rest While You Wait	61
Week 16	Rest That Builds	65
Week 17	Rest in Fulfilled Promises	69

Week 18	Rest Through Wholehearted Seeking	73
Week 19	Rest in the Darkness	77
Week 20	Rest in Hope	81
Week 21	Rest in Green Pastures	85
Week 22	Rest in the Refuge, Not the Escape	89
Week 23	Rest in the Secret Place	93
Week 24	Rest, My Soul	97
Week 25	Rest Is a Gift	101
Week 26	Rest Deferred for Devotion	105
Week 27	Rest in Being Known	109
Week 28	Rest After Obedience	113
Week 29	Rest in Wise Counsel	117
Week 30	Rest Isn't Relentlessness	121
Week 31	Rest Under His Rule	125
Week 32	Rest in the Spirit's Presence	129
Week 33	Rest Beneath His Hand	133
Week 34	Rest Refused, Grace Repeated	137
Week 35	Rest in Quiet Confidence	141
Week 36	Rest in Eternal Peace	145
Week 37	Rest Led by the Spirit	149
Week 38	Rest for the Weary and Faint	153
Week 39	Rest as a Sign of Belonging	157

Week 40	Rest at the End of the Journey	161
Week 41	Rest Beyond the Reach of Pride	165
Week 42	Rest Interrupted by Reality	169
Week 43	Rest Is a Holy Invitation	173
Week 44	Rest in the Revealed Messiah	177
Week 45	Rest in God's Comfort	181
Week 46	Rest in Righteous Justice	185
Week 47	Rest Received by Faith	189
Week 48	Rest Still Awaits	193
Week 49	Rest Is for Today	197
Week 50	Rest That Remains	201
Week 51	Rest from Our Work	205
Week 52	Rest That Follows Faithfulness	209
Finally	There is rest in belonging to the Lord.	213
	About the Author	217

INTRODUCTION

Then Jesus said, "Come to me, all of you who are weary and carry heavy burdens, and I will give you rest. Take my yoke upon you. Let me teach you, because I am humble and gentle at heart, and you will find rest for your souls. For my yoke is easy to bear, and the burden I give you is light" (Matthew 11:28-30).

Rest is hard to find lately. Even though it is intangible, the benefits are substantial. After a week off work, I realized that *rest* and *vacation* are not necessarily the same thing. On this scriptural journey, you will also discover some differences.

From Genesis to Revelation, the Sabbath and *rest* are connected on purpose. Recognizing the connection and applying rest appropriately may influence your life. That knowledge gave me the courage to release this offering.

The introductory scripture set me free, literally and figuratively. It was a lens through which I viewed decisions and activities. Not only did that verse help restore my soul, but it also affirmed my belief in 2 Timothy 3:16-17, which states, "All of Scripture is useful for teaching us what is true and for making us realize what is wrong in our lives. It corrects us when we are wrong and teaches us to do what is right. God uses it to prepare and equip his people to do every good work."

To complete the year, I selected fifty-two passages of scripture from Genesis to Revelation with a message on rest. I used the principles and purpose of Jubilee to present readers with the personal benefits of rest and to help them identify obstacles to their own spiritual "Jubilee". I encourage the practical application of rest in daily life. I urge you to allow enough time to reflect on each scripture and write your response in this journal. As you meditate on each week's devotion, I pray that you are renewed, refreshed, and revived.

Be Blessed!

Rev. Loretta

TODAY: Rest for the Soul

Scripture:

"Then Jesus said, 'Come to me, all of you who are weary and carry heavy burdens, and I will give you rest. Take my yoke upon you. Let me teach you, because I am humble and gentle at heart, and you will find rest for your souls. For my yoke is easy to bear, and the burden I give you is light.'"

— *Matthew 11:28–30 (NLT)*

Reflection:

Jesus doesn't say, "Fix yourself first." He says, "Come." Come with your weariness. Come with your burdens. Come with your questions, your failures, your fears. His invitation is not to a place, but to a Person.

We carry unseen burdens—expectations, regrets, and duties. But Jesus offers a different kind of burden: one that's light, one that fits, one that doesn't crush. His yoke is not about striving—it's about walking in step with Him.

Rest isn't just about sleeping or escape. It's about alignment. When we walk with Jesus, we learn from His gentleness. We move at His pace. We stop trying to earn love and start living in it.

If your soul feels tired, hear His voice today: "Come to Me." You don't have to carry it alone.

Prayer:

Jesus, I come to You with everything I'm carrying. Teach me to walk with You, not ahead of You. Help me release what's heavy and receive Your rest. Thank you for being gentle with my heart. Amen.

_____
_____
_____
_____
_____
_____
_____
_____
_____
_____
_____
_____
_____
_____
_____
_____
_____
_____
_____
_____

Journaling Prompt:

What burdens are you carrying today? Write them down and then write a prayer asking Jesus to help you release them.

_____
_____
_____
_____
_____
_____
_____
_____
_____
_____
_____
_____
_____
_____
_____
_____
_____
_____
_____
_____
_____
_____
_____
_____
_____
_____

WEEK 1: Rest After the Rain

Scripture:

"The floodwaters gradually receded from the earth. After 150 days, exactly five months from the time the flood began, the boat came to rest on the mountains of Ararat."

— *Genesis 8:3–4 (NLT)*

Reflection:

The storm had raged. The waters had risen. For months, Noah and his family floated in uncertainty, surrounded by silence and sky. But then—finally—the ark came to rest.

This wasn't just a physical pause. It was a spiritual milestone. After the chaos, God provided a place of stillness. A mountaintop. A moment to breathe. A sign that the worst was behind them.

Sometimes our lives feel like endless floods. We wait, we wonder, we pray for the waters to recede. But rest doesn't always come quickly. It comes gradually, like the floodwaters. And when it does, it's sacred.

God doesn't forget those who trust Him through the storm. He leads us to higher ground. Not just safety, but elevation. Not just survival, but renewal.

If you're still waiting for the waters to settle, hold on. Rest is coming. And when it does, it will be more than relief—it will be restoration.

Prayer:

Lord, thank You for being my anchor in the storm. Help me to trust Your timing and Your process. Lead me to the place of rest You've prepared for me. May I find peace, not just when the rain stops, but even while I wait. Amen.

Journaling Prompt:

Reflect on a season in your life that felt like a flood. How did God carry you through it? What did rest look like when it finally came?

WEEK 2: Rest Beneath the Shade

Scripture:

"Rest in the shade of this tree while water is brought to wash your feet."

— Genesis 18:4 (NLT)

Reflection:

In the heat of the day, Abraham welcomed three strangers with an invitation to rest. He didn't rush them or send them on their way. Instead, he offered shade, water, and comfort. This wasn't just kindness—it was sacred hospitality.

Rest often begins with an invitation. Sometimes, it's God inviting us to pause. Other times, it's us creating space for others to breathe. Abraham's gesture reminds us that rest can be simple: a quiet moment, a cool breeze, a place to sit and be.

In our busy lives, we often overlook the power of stillness. But God meets us in those shaded places. He refreshes us when we stop. He speaks when we listen. And He restores when we let go of the rush.

Whether you're the one offering rest or the one receiving it, know this: rest is holy. It's where healing begins. It's where God draws near.

Prayer:

Lord, thank You for the gift of rest. Help me to slow down and receive Your peace. Teach me to be like Abraham, welcoming, gentle, and aware of sacred moments. May I find shade in Your presence today. Amen.

Journaling Prompt:

Who in your life needs rest right now? How can you create space—physical or emotional—for them to pause and feel refreshed?

_____
_____
_____
_____
_____
_____
_____
_____
_____
_____
_____
_____
_____
_____
_____
_____
_____
_____
_____
_____
_____
_____

WEEK 3: Resting in Sacred Spaces

Scripture:

"At sundown he arrived at a good place to set up camp and stopped there for the night. Jacob found a stone to rest his head against and lay down to sleep."

— *Genesis 28:11 (NLT)*

Reflection:

Jacob was on the run—alone, uncertain, and far from home. Yet in his weariness, he stopped to rest. It wasn't a luxurious bed or a planned retreat. It was a stone pillow under the stars. But that night, in that humble place, Heaven opened.

Rest isn't just about physical recovery; it's often where revelation begins. When we pause, God speaks. When we sleep, He moves. Jacob's dream wasn't random—it was divine. And it came after he stopped.

How often do we rush past rest, thinking it's unproductive? But rest is sacred. It's where God meets us, renews us, and reminds us of His promises. Even in unfamiliar places, even with a stone for a pillow, God is nearby.

Don't underestimate the power of stopping. Your "good place" may not look perfect, but it may be exactly where God wants to speak.

Prayer:

Lord, teach me to embrace rest—not just for my body, but for my soul. Help me to slow down and trust that You are present even in the quiet. May my resting places become sacred spaces where I encounter You. Amen.

_____
_____
_____
_____
_____
_____
_____
_____
_____
_____
_____
_____
_____
_____
_____
_____
_____
_____
_____
_____
_____
_____
_____

Journaling Prompt:

Think of a time when rest led to clarity or peace. What did God reveal to you in that stillness?

_____
_____
_____
_____
_____
_____
_____
_____
_____
_____
_____
_____
_____
_____
_____
_____
_____
_____
_____
_____
_____
_____
_____
_____
_____

WEEK 4: Rest in His Presence

Scripture:

"The Lord replied, 'I will personally go with you, Moses, and I will give you rest—everything will be fine for you.'"

— Exodus 33:14 (NLT)

Reflection:

Moses was leading weary people through a wilderness of uncertainty. He didn't ask for a map or a miracle—he asked for God's presence. And God responded with a promise, *"I will personally go with you… I will give you rest."*

This kind of rest isn't found in circumstances. It's not the absence of struggle—it's the presence of God. When He walks with us, we can breathe deeper, trust more fully, and release the weight we carry.

God's rest is personal. It's not distant or abstract. It's Him—near, attentive, faithful. He doesn't send peace from afar; He brings it with Him. And when He says, *"Everything will be fine,"* it's not a vague reassurance—it's a divine guarantee.

If your heart feels restless, remember, you don't need all the answers. You need His presence. That's where rest begins.

Prayer:

Lord, thank You for going with me. I don't need to know every step—I need to know You're nearby. Help me to rest in Your presence today. Quiet my heart and remind me that everything will be fine because You are with me. Amen.

Journaling Prompt:

Where do you feel restless right now? Write a prayer inviting God's presence into that space and ask Him to give you rest.

WEEK 5: Reverence and Rest

Scripture:

"Each of you must show great respect for your mother and father, and you must always observe my Sabbath days of rest. I am the Lord your God."

— Leviticus 19:3 (NLT)

Reflection:

In this verse, God links two powerful commands: honoring our parents and observing the Sabbath rest. Both are rooted in reverence—one for those who gave us life, and one for the One who sustains it.

Sabbath isn't just a day off. It's a necessary pause that reminds us we're more than just our output. It's a weekly invitation to step back, breathe deeply, and remember who God is and who we are in Him.

When we honor the Sabbath, we declare that rest is holy. We trust that God is working even when we're not. We choose to worship instead of worry, to reflect instead of rush.

And just as we honor those who nurtured us, we honor the God who created us by resting in His presence. Reverence and rest go hand in hand. One shapes our relationships; the other restores our souls.

Prayer:

Lord, help me to live with reverence—for You, for my family, and for the gift of rest. Teach me to honor Your Sabbath not as a rule, but as a rhythm of renewal. May my rest be worship, and my worship be restful. Amen.

Journaling Prompt:

How do you observe rest in your life? What changes can you make to honor the Sabbath more intentionally?

WEEK 6: A Rhythm of Rest

Scripture:

"You have six days each week for your ordinary work, but the seventh day is a Sabbath day of complete rest, an official day for holy assembly. It is the Lord's Sabbath day, and it must be observed wherever you live."

— *Leviticus 23:3 (NLT)*

Reflection:

In a world that glorifies hustle, God calls us to pause. The Sabbath isn't just a break—it's a divine rhythm woven into creation itself. Six days of work, one day of rest. Not optional. Not outdated. Sacred.

This verse reminds us that rest is not just for the weary, it's for the obedient. It's a weekly invitation to step out of the ordinary and into the holy. To gather, to worship, to breathe. To remember that we are not machines—we are beloved children of God.

Sabbath rest is about trust. Trusting that the world won't fall apart if we stop. Trusting that God provides even when we pause. Trusting that our worth isn't tied to our productivity.

Wherever you live, whatever your schedule, God's invitation stands: come rest. Come worship. Be renewed.

Prayer:

Lord, thank You for the gift of Sabbath. Help me to honor Your rhythm of rest and worship. Teach me to slow down, to gather with others, and to find joy in Your presence. May my rest reflect my trust in You. Amen.

Journaling Prompt:

How do you currently observe the Sabbath? What changes can you make to embrace it more fully as a day of rest and worship?

WEEK 7: When the Land Rests Without Us

Scripture:

"Then at last the land will enjoy its neglected Sabbath years as it lies desolate while you are in exile in the land of your enemies. Then the land will finally rest and enjoy the Sabbaths it missed."

— *Leviticus 26:34 (NLT)*

Reflection:

God takes rest seriously—not just for people, but for the land itself. In this verse, He speaks of a time when the Israelites would be exiled, and only then would the land receive the rest it had been denied.

This is sobering. It reminds us that rest is not a suggestion, it's a command woven into creation. When we ignore it, something breaks. Our bodies wear down, our spirits grow weary, and even the spaces we inhabit suffer.

But there's grace in this truth. God doesn't just demand rest—He restores it. Even when we've neglected it, He makes a way for renewal. The land will rest. The soul will heal. The rhythm will return.

Let this verse be a gentle warning and a hopeful promise: rest matters. And when we honor it, we align ourselves with the Creator's design.

Prayer:

Lord, forgive me for the times I've ignored Your invitation to rest. Help me to honor the rhythms You've set—not just for my body, but for my life. Teach me to relax before I'm forced to. May I live in harmony with Your design. Amen.

_____
_____
_____
_____
_____
_____
_____
_____
_____
_____
_____
_____
_____
_____
_____
_____
_____
_____
_____
_____

Journaling Prompt:

Have you ever experienced burnout or exhaustion from neglecting rest? What changes can you make to restore balance and honor God's rhythm?

WEEK 8: Rest Along the Way

Scripture:

"They marched for three days after leaving the mountain of the Lord, with the Ark of the Lord's Covenant moving ahead of them to show them where to stop and rest."

— *Numbers 10:33 (NLT)*

Reflection:

The Israelites weren't wandering. Even in the wilderness, God was leading. The Ark of the Covenant didn't just symbolize His presence; it was His guidance, showing them where to stop and rest.

This verse reminds us that rest is not just a destination, it's part of the journey. God doesn't wait until we've "arrived" to offer renewal. He places rest along the way, knowing our limits, honoring our need to pause.

Sometimes, we push forward, thinking we must keep going to prove our strength. But God says, "Stop here. Rest now." He knows the terrain ahead. He knows what we need. And He lovingly leads us to places of refreshment.

If you're on a long journey—physically, emotionally, spiritually—watch for the signs. God is still guiding. And He's not just taking you somewhere; He's caring for you along the way.

Prayer:

Lord, thank You for leading me, not just to my destination, but through the journey. Help me to recognize the places You've prepared for me to rest. Help me pause at Your command and trust Your timing. Amen.

Journaling Prompt:

Where in your life do you feel like you're "marching"? How might God be inviting you to stop and rest—even if just for a moment?

_____
_____
_____
_____
_____
_____
_____
_____
_____
_____
_____
_____
_____
_____
_____
_____
_____
_____
_____
_____
_____
_____
_____
_____

WEEK 9: Rest in the Promised Place

Scripture:

"But you will soon cross the Jordan River and live in the land the Lord your God is giving you. When he gives you rest and security from all your enemies, you will live in safety. Then you must bring everything I command you—your burnt offerings, your sacrifices, your tithes, your sacred offerings, and your offerings to fulfill a vow—to the designated place of worship, the place the Lord your God chooses for his name to be honored."

— Deuteronomy 12:10–11 (NLT)

Reflection:

Rest isn't just relief—it's arrival. In this passage, God promises His people not only rest from their enemies, but a place to dwell in safety and worship. Rest and worship are deeply connected. When we're secure, we can offer ourselves fully to God.

This kind of rest is more than physical, spiritual, and emotional. It's the kind that comes after a long journey, a hard battle, or a season of wandering. It's the rest that says, *"You're home now."*

And in that place of rest, God invites us to respond—not with passivity, but with praise. We bring our offerings, our gratitude, our devotion. Rest becomes the foundation for worship, and worship becomes the expression of rest.

If you're longing for rest, know that God is leading you to a place of peace and purpose. And when you arrive, your worship will be deeper, richer, and more joyful than ever before.

Prayer:

Lord, thank You for the promise of rest and safety. Lead me to the place You've prepared for me—a place where I can dwell securely and worship freely. Help me to honor You, not just in the journey, but in the arrival. Amen.

Journaling Prompt:

What does "rest" look like in your life right now? How can you turn moments of rest into moments of worship?

WEEK 10: Remember the Promise of Rest

Scripture:

> "Remember what Moses, the servant of the Lord, commanded you: 'The Lord your God is giving you a place of rest. He has given you this land.'"
>
> — *Joshua 1:13 (NLT)*

Reflection:

As the Israelites prepared to enter the Promised Land, Joshua reminded them of something vital: *remember the promise.* God had already spoken through Moses. The land was theirs. The rest was coming. But in the midst of movement and battle, it was easy to forget.

We're not so different. Life gets busy. Challenges arise. And we forget what God has already said. We forget that rest is not just a future hope, it's a present promise. It's something God gives, not something we earn.

This verse calls us to pause and remember God is faithful. He keeps His word. The rest He offers is real peace for the soul, security for the heart, and a place to dwell in His presence.

And once we've received it, we're called to help others remember too. Rest is meant to be shared, not hoarded. It's a gift that multiplies when we live it out and speak it over others.

Prayer:

Lord, thank You for the promise of rest. Help me to remember what You've spoken, even when life feels uncertain. Teach me to live from a place of peace and to encourage others with Your faithfulness. Amen.

Journaling Prompt:

What promise of God do you need to remember today? Write it down and reflect on how it brings rest to your heart.

WEEK 11: Helping Others Find Rest

Scripture:

"Your wives, children, and livestock may remain here in the land Moses gave you on the east side of the Jordan. But your strong warriors, fully armed, must lead the other tribes across the Jordan to help them conquer their territory. Stay with them until the Lord gives them rest, as he has given you, and until they too possess the land the Lord your God is giving them."

— Joshua 1:14–15 (NLT)

Reflection:

The tribes of Reuben, Gad, and half of Manasseh had already received their inheritance. They had rested. But God called them to something more profound: to help their brothers find rest too.

This passage is a powerful reminder that rest isn't just personal, it's communal. When we've found peace, we're called to help others find theirs. When we've received our blessing, we're invited to be a blessing.

Rest is not the end of the journey—it's the beginning of service. God's people were never meant to settle while others still struggled. They were meant to stand together, fight together, and rest together.

Who around you is still in the battle? Who hasn't yet crossed their promise? Your strength, your story, your support might be the bridge they need.

Prayer:

Lord, thank You for the rest You've given me. Please show me how to use my strength to help others find theirs. Teach me to walk with those still in the fight and to be a source of encouragement and hope. May we all enter Your rest together. Amen.

Journaling Prompt:

Who in your life is still waiting for rest or a breakthrough? How can you walk alongside them in prayer, encouragement, or action?

_____
_____
_____
_____
_____
_____
_____
_____
_____
_____
_____
_____
_____
_____
_____
_____
_____
_____
_____
_____
_____
_____
_____

WEEK 12: Rest on Every Side

Scripture:

"And the Lord gave them rest on every side, just as he had solemnly promised their ancestors. None of their enemies could stand against them, for the Lord helped them conquer all their enemies."

— *Joshua 21:44 (NLT)*

Reflection:

After years of wandering, battles, and waiting, the Israelites finally experienced what God had promised: rest on every side. Not partial peace. Not temporary relief. Complete rest—secured by God's faithfulness.

This kind of rest is more than a break from conflict. It's the fruit of obedience, trust, and perseverance. It's the kind of peace that settles deep into the soul, knowing that God has kept His word.

We all long for rest like this. Rest from anxiety. Rest from striving. Rest from the battles we fight in silence. And this verse reminds us that God is able. He doesn't just promise rest—He delivers it. Not because we're strong, but because He is.

If you're still in the fight, hold on. Rest is coming. And when it does, it will surround you. It will be unmistakable. It will be God's signature of victory over your life.

Prayer:

Lord, thank You for being faithful to Your promises. I trust that You are leading me toward rest on every side. Help me to walk in obedience and faith, knowing that You are my defender and my peace. Amen.

_____
_____
_____
_____
_____
_____
_____
_____
_____
_____
_____
_____
_____
_____
_____
_____
_____
_____
_____
_____

Journaling Prompt:

Where have you seen God give you rest in the past? What areas of your life still need His peace? Write a prayer of trust, believing He will bring rest in His perfect time.

WEEK 13: Rest Beyond Revenge

Scripture:

"Because you did this," Samson vowed, "I won't rest until I take my revenge on you!"

— Judges 15:7 (NLT)

Reflection:

Samson's words are raw and reactive. Fueled by betrayal and anger, he declares that rest will only come after revenge. It's a sentiment many of us understand—when we've been hurt, wronged, or misunderstood, rest feels impossible until justice is served.

But this verse also reveals a more profound truth: revenge is a restless pursuit. It keeps us stirred up, focused on payback rather than peace. Samson's vow shows how easily we can tie our sense of rest to unresolved pain.

God offers a different path. His rest isn't earned through retaliation—it's received through release. When we surrender our need to get even, we make space for healing. When we trust God to be our defender, we find rest, not in resolution, but in His righteousness.

Rest doesn't mean ignoring injustice. It means refusing to let it consume us. It means choosing peace over bitterness, and trusting that God sees, knows, and will act in His perfect time.

Prayer:

Lord, help me let go of the need for revenge. Teach me to rest in Your justice and trust Your timing. Heal the places in me that ache for resolution and fill them with Your peace. Amen.

Journaling Prompt:

Is there someone or something you've struggled to let go of? Write about how that tension has affected your rest and ask God to help you release it.

WEEK 14: Rest in the Rhythm of Grace

Scripture:

> *"She asked me this morning if she could gather grain behind the harvesters. She has been hard at work ever since, except for a few minutes' rest in the shelter."*
>
> — *Ruth 2:7 (NLT)*

Reflection: Ruth's story demonstrates quiet strength. She didn't demand attention or entitlement—she asked to gather what was left behind. And then she worked. Faithfully. Humbly. Tirelessly. But even with her diligence, she paused for rest.

This verse reminds us that rest is not weakness—it's wisdom. Ruth didn't stop because she was lazy. She stopped because she was human. And in that brief pause, she honored the rhythm of grace.

We often push ourselves to prove our worth, forgetting that God values both our effort and our restoration. Ruth's rest wasn't extravagant—it was a few minutes in the shelter. But it was enough. Enough to breathe. Enough to be renewed. Enough to keep going.

God sees your labor. He honors your faithfulness. And He invites you to rest—not just when the work is done, but during it. Even a few minutes in His shelter can restore your soul.

Prayer:

Lord, thank You for seeing my quiet efforts. Please help me to embrace rest as part of my rhythm, not a reward I must earn. Teach me to pause in Your presence and find renewal in Your grace. Amen.

Journaling Prompt:

Where in your daily routine can you carve out moments of rest? What would it look like to pause in God's shelter, even briefly?

WEEK 15: Rest While You Wait

Scripture:

"Then Naomi said to her, 'Just be patient, my daughter, until we hear what happens. The man won't rest until he has settled things today.'"

— Ruth 3:18 (NLT)

Reflection:

Ruth had done all she could. She had followed Naomi's guidance, approached Boaz with humility, and made her intentions known. Now, she had to wait. And Naomi's words were both tender and wise *"Just be patient."*

Waiting is one of the most complicated forms of rest. It asks us to trust when we can't see, to be still when we want to act, and to believe that someone else—God Himself—is working on our behalf.

Boaz wouldn't rest until Ruth's future was secured. In the same way, our Redeemer doesn't rest until our restoration is complete. Jesus intercedes, advocates, and moves on our behalf—even when we're called to be still.

Rest in waiting isn't passive; it's faith-filled. It's choosing peace over panic, trust over turmoil. It's believing that God is settling things, even when we don't yet see the outcome.

Prayer:

Lord, help me to rest while I wait. Teach me to trust that You are working behind the scenes, settling things I cannot control. Give me patience, peace, and the assurance that You are my faithful Redeemer. Amen.

Journaling Prompt:

What are you waiting for right now? Write about the emotions that come with waiting and ask God to help you rest in His timing.

WEEK 16: Rest That Builds

Scripture:

"When King David was settled in his palace and the Lord had given him rest from all the surrounding enemies, the king summoned Nathan the prophet. 'Look,' David said, 'I am living in a beautiful cedar palace, but the Ark of God is out there in a tent!' Nathan replied to the king, 'Go ahead and do whatever you have in mind, for the Lord is with you.'"

— *2 Samuel 7:1–3 (NLT)*

Reflection:

David had finally entered a season of rest. No more battles. No more running. He was settled, secure, and surrounded by peace. And what did he do with that rest? He turned his heart toward God.

This passage reveals a beautiful truth: rest isn't just for recovery, it's for reflection. When the noise quiets and the pressure lifts, we're invited to consider how we can honor God with what we've been given.

David's desire to build a house for the Lord came from a place of gratitude. He looked around at his blessings and realized that God deserved more than a tent. His rest stirred worship—his peace birthed purpose.

What we do with our rest matters. It's not just a pause, it's a platform—a chance to dream, to serve, to build something that glorifies God.

Prayer:

Lord, thank You for the seasons of rest You provide. Help me use them not just for comfort, but also for calling. Stir my heart to honor You with what I have, and to build something that reflects Your goodness. Amen.

Journaling Prompt:

What has God given you in seasons of rest? How might you use that peace to create something that honors Him?

WEEK 17: Rest in Fulfilled Promises

Scripture:

"Praise the Lord who has given rest to his people Israel, just as he promised. Not one word has failed of all the wonderful promises he gave through his servant Moses."

— *1 Kings 8:56 (NLT)*

Reflection:

Solomon's words echo with awe and gratitude. After generations of wandering, waiting, and warfare, the people of Israel had finally entered into rest—not just physical peace, but the deep assurance that God had kept His word.

This verse is a powerful reminder that *God's promises never fail.* Not one word. Even when the journey feels long, even when the waiting is hard, even when the outcome seems uncertain—He is faithful.

Rest comes when we stop striving and start trusting. It's not just the absence of trouble—it's the presence of fulfillment. When we see God's hand in our story, we can exhale. We can worship. We can rest.

If you're still waiting on a promise, let this verse be your anchor. God has not forgotten. His timing is perfect. And when the promise is fulfilled, it will bring rest to your soul and praise to your lips.

Prayer:

Lord, thank You for being faithful to every promise. Help me to rest in Your Word, even when I'm still waiting. Teach me to trust Your timing and celebrate Your goodness. May my life be a testimony to Your unfailing love. Amen.

Journaling Prompt:

What promise from God are you holding on to right now? Write it down and reflect on how His past faithfulness gives you confidence to rest in the present.

_____
_____
_____
_____
_____
_____
_____
_____
_____
_____
_____
_____
_____
_____
_____
_____
_____
_____
_____
_____
_____
_____
_____

WEEK 18: Rest Through Wholehearted Seeking

Scripture:

"All Judah rejoiced over the oath because they had sworn it with all their heart. They earnestly sought after God, and they found him. And the Lord gave them rest from their enemies on every side."

— *2 Chronicles 15:15 (NLT)*

Reflection:

There's a kind of rest that only comes after surrender. In this verse, the people of Judah didn't just make a promise; they made it with *all their hearts*. They sought God earnestly, and He responded with presence, peace, and protection.

This is the rhythm of renewal: repentance, pursuit, and rest. When we turn to God with everything—no holding back, no half-heartedness—He meets us with grace. And not just grace for the moment, but rest on every side.

Rest isn't just a gift, it's a response. It flows from a relationship. When our hearts are aligned with God, peace follows. Not because life is perfect, but because our souls are anchored.

If you've been longing for rest, consider this: Are you seeking Him with your whole heart? Because when we do, He is always found. And when He is found, rest is never far behind.

Prayer:

Lord, I want to seek You with all my heart. Remove anything that divides my devotion. Help me to pursue You earnestly and trust that You will meet me with peace. Thank You for the rest that comes from knowing You. Amen.

Journaling Prompt:

What does wholehearted seeking look like in your life? Are there areas where you've held back? Write a prayer of surrender and ask God to bring rest as you draw near.

WEEK 19: Rest in the Darkness

Scripture:

"I have no peace, no quietness. I have no rest; only trouble comes."

— Job 3:26 (NLT)

Reflection:

Job's words are heavy. They echo the ache of a soul undone by grief. In this moment, rest feels unreachable. Peace is absent. Trouble is relentless. And yet—this verse is sacred because it tells the truth.

Rest isn't always easy to find. There are seasons when sorrow drowns out silence, when pain interrupts peace, when even sleep feels like a stranger. Job's lament reminds us that God welcomes honesty. He doesn't flinch at our despair. He meets us in it.

This kind of rest isn't about resolution or presence. Even when Job couldn't feel peace, God was nearby. Even when rest was gone, God was listening. And though Job didn't know it yet, restoration was coming.

If you're in a season where rest feels far away, take heart: God is not. He is with you in the darkness. He holds space for your sorrow. And He promises that trouble will not have the final word.

Prayer:

Lord, I offer my unrest to You. My weariness. My sorrow. Thank You for meeting me here, even when I have no words. Help me to trust that You are near, and that rest will return in Your time. Amen.

Journaling Prompt:

Write honestly about a time when rest felt impossible. What did you learn about God in that season? What do you need from Him today?

WEEK 20: Rest in Hope

Scripture:

"Having hope will give you courage. You will be protected and will rest in safety."

— Job 11:18 (NLT)

Reflection:

Hope is more than wishful thinking—it's a spiritual anchor. In this verse, Zophar speaks to Job, offering a glimpse of what hope can restore: courage, protection, and rest. While his theology may have been imperfect, this truth remains—hope leads to rest.

When we lose hope, rest feels impossible. Our minds race, our hearts ache, and fear takes over. But when hope is present, it steadies us. It whispers, *"You're not alone. God is still working."* And that assurance becomes a shelter.

Rest in safety doesn't mean life is free from hardship. It means our souls are held securely in God's hands. Hope gives us the courage to face uncertainty, knowing that our refuge is not in outcomes, but in the One who holds them.

If you're weary, ask God to renew your hope. Let it be the light that leads you to rest—not just for your body, but for your spirit.

Prayer:

Lord, restore my hope today. Let it be the courage I need and the rest I long for. Help me to trust that You are my protector, and that I can safely rest in Your promises. Amen.

Journaling Prompt:

How do you define hope at this moment? Describe an occasion when hope provided you with courage. Reflect on how that strength can be renewed today.

WEEK 21: Rest in Green Pastures

Scripture:

"He lets me rest in green meadows; He leads me beside peaceful streams."

— Psalm 23:2 (NLT)

Reflection:

This verse is a breath of fresh air. It paints a picture of rest, not as escape, but as invitation. The Shepherd doesn't drive us—He *leads* us. He doesn't demand rest—He *lets* us rest. And where does He take us? To green meadows and peaceful streams. Places of nourishment. Places of stillness.

In a world of noise and motion, this kind of rest feels rare. But it's always available. The Shepherd knows exactly where your soul can breathe again. He doesn't rush you past the meadow—He settles you there. He doesn't push you into the stream—He walks beside you.

This rest is not earned. It's received. It's not a luxury, it's a promise. And it's not just physical, spiritual. It's the kind of rest that restores your soul, quiets your mind, and reminds you that you are deeply loved.

Let Him lead you today. Let Him settle you in the meadow. Let Him speak peace over your heart.

Prayer:

Lord, thank You for being my Shepherd. Lead me to the places where my soul can rest. Help me to slow down, to listen, and to receive Your peace. May I find renewal beside Your still waters. Amen.

Journaling Prompt:

What does your "green meadow" look like right now? Where do you feel most at peace with God? Write about how you can make space for that kind of rest this week.

_____
_____
_____
_____
_____
_____
_____
_____
_____
_____
_____
_____
_____
_____
_____
_____
_____
_____
_____
_____
_____
_____
_____
_____
_____

WEEK 22: Rest in the Refuge, Not the Escape

Scripture:

"Oh, that I had wings like a dove; then I would fly away and rest!"

— Psalm 55:6 (NLT)

Reflection:

David's cry is achingly familiar. During betrayal and turmoil, he longs to escape—to fly away, to find rest somewhere far from the pain. It's a raw, honest moment. And it reminds us that even the faithful sometimes feel overwhelmed.

We've all had days like this. Days when the weight is too much, when the noise is too loud, when the heart says, *"If only I could disappear."* But rest isn't found in running—it's found in refuge. And God is that refuge.

The wings David longs for are symbolic of peace, of freedom, of safety. And while we may not sprout feathers and flee, we are invited to spread the wings of prayer, worship, and trust. To rise above the chaos—not by escaping it, but by anchoring ourselves in the One who calms it.

God doesn't always remove the storm, but He always offers shelter. And in His presence, we find rest—not far away, but right where we are.

Prayer:

Lord, when I feel like flying away, remind me that You are my refuge. Help me to rest, not in escape, but in Your presence. Give me peace in the middle of the storm and strength to stay grounded in You. Amen.

Journaling Prompt:

Have you ever longed to escape a situation or season? Write about that feeling and reflect on how God might be inviting you to find rest in Him instead.

WEEK 23: Rest in the Secret Place

Scripture:

"Those who live in the shelter of the Most High will find rest in the shadow of the Almighty."

— *Psalm 91:1 (NLT)*

Reflection:

This verse is a sanctuary. It speaks of a place, not just to visit, but to *live*—a shelter, a shadow, a refuge. It's not about escaping the world but abiding in the One who holds it.

Rest in the shadow of the Almighty is not passive—it's intentional. It's choosing to dwell, to remain, to trust. The secret place isn't hidden from us—it's hidden *from* us—a place of peace, protection, and presence.

When life feels loud and uncertain, this verse invites us to lean in. To rest, not in answers, but in intimacy. To find comfort, not in control, but in surrender. The shadow of the Almighty is not a dark place; it's a covering. A shield. A quiet space where our souls can breathe.

If you've been searching for rest, step into the shelter. Stay a while. Let His presence be your peace.

Prayer:

Lord, draw me into Your shelter. Help me to dwell—not just visit—in Your presence. Let Your shadow be my refuge, and Your nearness my rest. Teach me to abide in You, moment by moment. Amen.

Journaling Prompt:

What does "living in the shelter of the Most High" look like for you? Write about how you can cultivate that kind of abiding rest in your daily life.

WEEK 24: Rest, My Soul

Scripture:

"Let my soul be at rest again, for the Lord has been good to me."

— Psalm 116:7 (NLT)

Reflection:

Sometimes, we need to speak directly to our own soul. That's what the psalmist does here—not with denial, but with remembrance. He calls his soul back to rest by recalling the goodness of God.

This verse is a gentle command, a sacred self-reminder: *"Rest again."* Not for the first time, but again. Because life unsettles us, circumstances shake us. But God's goodness remains. And that goodness is the anchor that steadies us.

Rest isn't just a feeling, it's a decision. A declaration. A return. When we remember what God has done—how He's rescued, healed, provided, comforted—we can invite our souls to settle again. Not because everything is perfect, but because He is faithful.

If your soul feels stirred up today, speak these words aloud *"Let my soul be at rest again."* Let them echo through your heart. Let them remind you of the goodness that never left.

Prayer:

Lord, You have been so good to me. Help me to remember Your faithfulness and speak peace over my soul. Please show me how to find rest continually. You are my refuge and my reason to breathe deeply. Amen.

Journaling Prompt:

Write a list of ways God has been good to you. Then, write a personal prayer inviting your soul to rest again in that goodness.

WEEK 25: Rest Is a Gift

Scripture:

"It is useless for you to work so hard from early morning until late at night, anxiously working for food to eat; for God gives rest to his loved ones."

— Psalm 127:2 (NLT)

Reflection:

This verse gently confronts our culture of hustle. It reminds us that anxiously striving—working endlessly, worrying constantly—is not the way of the Kingdom. God doesn't reward burnout. He gives rest.

Rest is not earned through effort. It's received through trust. When we believe that God is our provider, we stop grasping and start breathing. We lay down the need to control and pick up the peace He offers.

Sleep, in this verse, is more than physical or spiritual. It's the kind of rest that comes from knowing you are loved, held, and secure. It's the kind of rest that silences fear and soothes the soul.

If you've been working hard and worrying harder, hear this truth: God gives rest to His beloved. That includes you. You don't have to prove anything. You are already loved. And the rest is waiting.

Prayer:

Lord, thank You for loving me enough to give me rest. Help me to release anxious striving and receive Your peace. Teach me to trust Your provision and sleep in the safety of Your love. Amen.

Journaling Prompt:

Where in your life are you striving anxiously? Write about what it would look like to surrender that area to God and receive His rest instead.

WEEK 26: Rest Deferred for Devotion

Scripture:

"I will not go home; I will not let myself rest."

— *Psalm 132:3 (NLT)*

Reflection:

This verse captures a moment of holy resolve. The psalmist, echoing David's vow, refuses rest until a dwelling place is made for God. It's a declaration of devotion—of putting God's presence above personal comfort.

There are seasons when rest is delayed, not out of neglect, but out of purpose. When the Spirit stirs us to build, to pray, to create, to seek, our rest becomes "a gentle surrender in the midst of purposeful striving"

But even in times of urgency, God's heart is not for burnout. He honors our passion, but He also invites us to balance. To know when to press in and when to lie down. David's vow led to the building of the temple—but it also led to a legacy of worship and rest for generations.

If you're in a season of spiritual drive, remember: God sees your devotion. He honors your sacrifice. But He also whispers, *"Come home. Let yourself rest."* Because rest is not the absence of passion—it's the rhythm of grace.

Prayer:

Lord, I want to honor You with my devotion. Teach me when to press forward and when to pause. Please help me to build from a place of rest, not exhaustion. Let my urgency be rooted in love and my rest be received with joy. Amen.

Journaling Prompt:

Is there an area of your life where you've been deferring rest for the sake of purpose? Write about how God might be inviting you to balance passion with peace.

WEEK 27: Rest in Being Known

Scripture:

"You see me when I travel and when I rest at home. You know everything I do."

— *Psalm 139:3 (NLT)*

Reflection:

There's a deep peace in being known. Not just noticed, but truly seen. This verse reminds us that God watches over every movement—our going out, our coming in, our work, our rest. Nothing escapes His attention. And nothing about us is hidden.

In a world that often demands performance, it's easy to feel unseen unless we're producing or proving. But God's gaze is gentle. He sees us when we're active and when we're still. When we're strong and when we're weary. His knowing is not surveillance—it's love.

Rest comes when we stop trying to be enough and receive the truth: *we are already known and loved.* Whether we're traveling through busy seasons or resting quietly at home, God is with us. And His presence is our peace.

Let this verse be a reminder that you don't have to earn God's attention. You already have it. And in that knowing, you can truly rest.

Prayer:

Lord, thank You for seeing me—always. In motion and in stillness, You are nearby. Help me to rest in the comfort of being fully known and deeply loved. Let Your presence be my peace. Amen.

Journaling Prompt:

Where do you feel most seen by God? Write about a moment when you felt known and reflect on how that awareness brings rest to your soul.

WEEK 28: Rest After Obedience

Scripture:

"Don't put it off; do it now! Don't rest until you do."

— *Proverbs 6:4 (NLT)*

Reflection:

This verse is a call to action. It speaks to moments when rest must wait—when obedience must come first. In context, it urges the reader to resolve a mistake, to free themselves from entanglement. It's not about frantic striving—it's about faithful urgency.

Sometimes, rest is delayed because unfinished business tugs at our spirits. This discussion warrants our attention; we need to make it right. A step of obedience we've been avoiding. And until we act, rest remains elusive.

But here's the grace: God doesn't ask for perfection—He asks for movement. When we respond to His prompting, even imperfectly, peace follows. Rest comes, not just from stopping, but from following His instructions and trusting Him with the result.

If something's been weighing on your heart, don't put it off. Please do it now. Not out of fear, but out of faith. Because rest is waiting on the other side of obedience.

Prayer:

Lord, show me what I've been putting off. Give me courage to act, to obey, to respond to Your voice. Help me to trust that rest will follow when I walk in Your will. Amen.

Journaling Prompt:

Is there something God has been nudging you to do? Write about what's holding you back and how taking that step might lead to deeper rest.

WEEK 29: Rest in Wise Counsel

Scripture:

"Get all the advice and instruction you can, so you will be wise the rest of your life."

— Proverbs 19:20 (NLT)

Reflection:

Wisdom is not a one-time gift—it's a lifelong pursuit. This verse reminds us that rest and wisdom are deeply connected. When we seek godly counsel and instruction, we're not just gathering knowledge; we're building a foundation for peace.

Rest doesn't come from knowing everything; it comes from knowing where to turn. When we humble ourselves to receive advice, we release the pressure of figuring it all out alone. We open our hearts to guidance and, in doing so, find clarity, direction, and rest.

God often speaks through others—mentors, friends, scripture, even quiet nudges in prayer. When we listen, we grow. And when we grow, we walk more confidently, more peacefully, more wisely.

If you've been wrestling with a decision or carrying confusion, consider this: rest might be waiting in the wisdom of someone you trust. Don't be afraid to ask, to learn, to receive.

Prayer:

Lord, help me to seek and receive wise counsel. Give me a teachable heart and ears that listen. Lead me to voices that reflect Your truth and let Your wisdom bring rest to my soul. Amen.

Journaling Prompt:

Who are the wise voices in your life? Write about a time when good advice brought you peace. Reflect on how you can continue to grow through instruction.

WEEK 30: Rest Isn't Relentlessness

Scripture:

"They never stumble or lag behind; they are never stopped by fatigue. They never sleep. Not a moment's rest."

— *Isaiah 5:27 (NLT)*

Reflection:

This verse describes a tireless army—disciplined, relentless, and unceasing. But it's not a picture of peace. It's a warning: constant motion without rest has consequences.

In our own lives, we sometimes wear exhaustion like a badge. We push through fatigue, ignore the signs, and convince ourselves that rest is weakness. But Isaiah's imagery reminds us, relentless motion isn't holy—it's haunting.

God never designed us to live without pause. Even He rested. Even Jesus withdrew. Rest is not a break from purpose—it's part of it. Without it, we stumble. We lag. We lose sight of grace.

This verse invites us to reflect: Are we marching through life without margin? Are we chasing goals without grounding in God's rhythm? Because true strength is found not in constant motion, but in sacred stillness.

Prayer:

Lord, protect me from the lie that rest is failure. Teach me to pause, to breathe, to trust that You work even when I stop. Help me to live in Your rhythm, not the world's rush. Amen.

Journaling Prompt:

Have you ever felt like you were living without a moment's rest? Write about what drove that season, and how God might be inviting you to step into a gentler pace.

WEEK 31: Rest Under His Rule

Scripture:

> *"For a child is born to us, a son is given to us. The government will rest on his shoulders. And he will be called: Wonderful Counselor, Mighty God, Everlasting Father, Prince of Peace."*
>
> *— Isaiah 9:6 (NLT)*

Reflection:

This verse is a declaration of hope. In the midst of darkness, Isaiah speaks of a child—a gift—who will carry the weight of the world and usher in a kingdom of peace. And not just any peace, but the kind that flows from divine wisdom, strength, and eternal love.

The government resting on His shoulders means we don't have to carry it ourselves. The burdens of leadership, decision-making, and control are not ours to bear alone. Jesus, our Prince of Peace, holds it all. And in His reign, rest is not just possible, it's promised.

Each name in this verse is an invitation:

- *Wonderful Counselor*—rest in His wisdom.
- *Mighty God*—rest in His strength.
- *Everlasting Father*—rest in His love.
- *Prince of Peace*—rest in His presence.

If your heart feels heavy today, remember this: the child has come. The Son has been given. And His shoulders are strong enough to carry what you cannot.

Prayer:

Jesus, You are my Prince of Peace. Thank You for carrying what I cannot. Help me to rest in Your wisdom, strength, love, and presence. Let Your reign bring peace to my heart today. Amen.

_____
_____
_____
_____
_____
_____
_____
_____
_____
_____
_____
_____
_____
_____
_____
_____
_____
_____
_____
_____
_____
_____

Journaling Prompt:

Which name of Jesus in this verse speaks most deeply to you right now? Write about how that aspect of His character invites you into rest.

WEEK 32: Rest in the Spirit's Presence

Scripture:

"And the Spirit of the Lord will rest on him—the Spirit of wisdom and understanding, the Spirit of counsel and might, the Spirit of knowledge and the fear of the Lord."

— Isaiah 11:2 (NLT)

Reflection:

This verse speaks of Jesus—the promised branch from David's line—anointed with the fullness of God's Spirit. And what a Spirit it is: wisdom, understanding, counsel, might, knowledge, reverence. Not just power, but peace. Not just authority, but rest.

The Spirit of the Lord *rests* on Him. That word is gentle, intentional, sacred. It's not rushed or forced—it's settled. And because the Spirit rests on Jesus, we can rest in Him.

When we feel confused, the Spirit offers wisdom. When we feel weak, He brings might. When we feel uncertain, He gives counsel. And when we feel distant, He draws us near in holy reverence.

Rest isn't just about stopping—it's about being filled. And the Spirit fills us with everything we need to walk wisely, live boldly, and rest securely.

Prayer:

Holy Spirit, rest on me as You rested on Jesus. Please fill me with wisdom, understanding, and strength. Teach me to live in reverence and peace, and to find rest in Your presence every day. Amen.

Journaling Prompt:

Which aspect of the Spirit in this verse do you need most today—wisdom, understanding, counsel, might, knowledge, or reverence? Write about how that gift could bring rest to your soul.

WEEK 33: Rest Beneath His Hand

Scripture:

"The Lord's hand of blessing will rest on Jerusalem. Moab will be crushed as straw is trampled down and left to rot."

— Isaiah 25:10 (NLT)

Reflection:

This verse paints a vivid contrast—blessing and judgment, rest and ruin. For Jerusalem, the Lord's hand brings peace, protection, and favor. For Moab, resistance to God leads to downfall. It's a sober reminder that rest is not just a feeling, it's a placement. It's about *where* we dwell and *whose* hand we trust.

To rest under God's hand is to live in surrender. It's to receive His covering, His guidance, His grace. It's not passive, it's powerful. Because when His hand rests on us, no enemy can stand. No fear can rule. No striving is needed.

This verse also reminds us that rest is a result of a relationship. Jerusalem's blessing came from belonging. And we, too, are invited to belong—to be part of the city of peace, the people of promise, the ones who rest beneath His hand.

If you've felt exposed or vulnerable, let this truth settle in: God's hand of blessing *rests* on you. Not briefly, not conditionally—but securely.

Prayer:

Lord, I want to live beneath Your hand of blessing. Cover me with Your peace, protect me with Your presence, and teach me to rest in Your strength. Let my life be rooted in You. Amen.

Journaling Prompt:

What does it mean to you to rest under God's hand? Write about a time when you felt His protection or favor. Reflect on how that shaped your sense of peace.

WEEK 34: Rest Refused, Grace Repeated

Scripture:

"God told them, 'This is the place of rest; let the weary rest here. This is a place of quiet.' But they would not listen."

— Isaiah 28:12 (NLT)

Reflection:

This verse is both tender and heartbreaking. God offers rest—clearly, lovingly, directly. He sees the weariness of His people and points to the quiet place. But they refuse. They would not listen.

How often do we do the same? We hear the invitation to slow down, to trust, to breathe—but we keep pushing. We ignore the whisper and chase the noise. And yet, God keeps offering. His grace repeats. His rest remains available.

The tragedy isn't in the weariness—it's in the refusal. But the hope is this: even when we've ignored Him, He still calls. The place of rest is still open. The quiet still waits.

If you've been running past the invitation, pause. Listen again. The Spirit is still saying, *"Let the weary rest here."* And you are welcome.

Prayer:

Lord, forgive me for the times I've ignored Your invitation to rest. Help me to listen, to respond, to receive the quiet You offer. Let me be among those who hear and come. Amen.

Journaling Prompt:

Have you ever sensed God inviting you to rest but struggled to accept it? Write about what held you back and how you might respond differently today.

WEEK 35: Rest in Quiet Confidence

Scripture:

"My people will live in safety, quietly at home. They will be at rest."

— *Isaiah 32:18 (NLT)*

Reflection:

This verse is a vision of peace fulfilled. It speaks of a time when God's people dwell in safety—not just physically, but spiritually. Quietly, at home. At rest. It's not the rest of escape, but the rest of arrival. The kind that comes after righteousness has done its work.

Isaiah 32 describes a coming reign of justice in which the Spirit is poured out and the wilderness becomes fertile. And in that renewal, rest is the reward. Not just for individuals, but for communities. For *His people*.

This rest is marked by quietness—not silence, but serenity. It's the kind of peace that settles deep, that doesn't need to prove or perform. It's the rest of knowing you're held, covered, and secure.

If your soul has been noisy or unsettled, let this verse be a promise: God desires for you to live in safety, to dwell quietly, to rest deeply. And that rest is rooted in righteousness—not yours, but His.

Prayer:

Lord, thank You for the promise of quiet rest. Help me to dwell in Your righteousness and live in the safety of Your presence. Let my home—my heart—be a place of peace. Amen.

Journaling Prompt:

What does "quietly at home" mean to you spiritually? Write about how God might be inviting you to settle into a deeper place of rest and safety.

WEEK 36: Rest in Eternal Peace

Scripture:

"For those who follow godly paths will rest in peace when they die."

— Isaiah 57:2 (NLT)

Reflection:

This verse offers a quiet assurance, a promise that godly living leads to godly rest, even beyond this life. It's not a verse of fear, but of fulfillment. A gentle reminder that the journey of righteousness ends not in chaos, but in peace.

For those who walk with God, death is not the end—it's the beginning of eternal rest. Not just sleep, but *shalom*—wholeness, safety, restoration. It's the kind of peace that cannot be shaken, because it's held in the hands of the Eternal One.

This verse also invites reflection on how we live now. Are we walking godly paths? Are we cultivating peace in our daily choices, relationships, and rhythms? Because the rest we long for later begins with the surrender we offer today.

If you've lost someone who walked with God, let this verse comfort you. Their rest is real. Their peace is complete. And if you're weary of the journey, let it remind you: every step of faith is leading you home.

Prayer:

Lord, thank You for the promise of eternal peace. Help me to walk in Your way today, trusting that rest awaits me in Your presence. Let my life reflect Your righteousness, and my heart rest in Your hope. Amen.

Journaling Prompt:

Reflect on what eternal rest means to you. Write about how the promise of peace after death shapes the way you live and seek rest now.

WEEK 37: Rest Led by the Spirit

Scripture:

"As with cattle going down into a peaceful valley, the Spirit of the Lord gave them rest. You led your people, Lord, and gained a magnificent reputation."

— *Isaiah 63:14 (NLT)*

Reflection:

This verse is a tender image of divine guidance. Like cattle descending into a quiet valley, God's people are led into rest—not by force, but by the Spirit. It's a picture of trust, of rhythm, of surrender. The valley isn't just peaceful, it's purposeful. It's where rest is found.

The Spirit of the Lord gives rest. Not just physical relief, but soul-deep renewal. And this rest is part of God's reputation—it reveals His character. He's not only mighty in battle or majestic in glory—He's gentle in leading. He's known for bringing His people home.

If you've been wandering or weary, this verse is an invitation: let the Spirit lead you. Let Him guide you into the valley, into the quiet, into the rest that reflects God's goodness. You don't have to find it on your own. You only have to follow.

Prayer:

Spirit of the Lord, lead me into rest. Guide me gently, like a shepherd, into the peaceful valley of Your presence. Let my life reflect Your care and let my rest bring glory to Your name. Amen.

Journaling Prompt:

Where is the Spirit leading you right now? Write about how you can follow more closely, and what kind of rest you hope to find in the valley.

WEEK 38: Rest for the Weary and Faint

Scripture:

"The people will live in Judah and its towns again. And I will refresh those who are weary and give rest to the faint."

— *Jeremiah 31:24–25 (NLT)*

Reflection:

This passage is a promise of return and renewal. After exile and sorrow, God speaks restoration: the towns will be inhabited again, and the weary will be refreshed. It's a vision of hope for those who feel displaced—physically, emotionally, spiritually.

God doesn't just bring His people back—He brings them back *better*. He doesn't just rebuild cities—He revives souls. And for those who are faint, He offers rest. Not just sleep, but strength. Not just pause, but peace.

This verse reminds us that weariness is not failure; it's a signal—a sacred invitation to be refreshed by the One who never grows tired. When we're faint, He doesn't shame us—He lifts us. When we're weary, He doesn't push us—He carries us.

If you've been feeling worn down, let this promise settle in: God sees you. He knows your fatigue. And He is ready to refresh and restore.

Prayer:

Lord, thank You for Your promise to refresh the weary and give rest to the faint. I received your renewal today. Restore what's been depleted and help me to dwell again in the peace of Your presence. Amen.

Journaling Prompt:

Where have you felt faint or weary lately? Write about how God might be inviting you to return, be refreshed, and rest in Him.

WEEK 39: Rest as a Sign of Belonging

Scripture:

> *"And I gave them my Sabbath days of rest as a sign between them and me. It was to remind them that I am the Lord, who had set them apart to be holy."*
>
> — *Ezekiel 20:12 (NLT)*

Reflection:

Rest involves more than simple rhythm. It is a relationship. In this verse, God describes the Sabbath as a *sign* between Him and His people. A sacred marker of belonging. A weekly reminder that they are set apart, chosen, holy.

The Sabbath was never meant to be a burden—it was a gift. A pause that pointed to presence. A day that declared, *"You are mine, and I am yours."* In resting, the people remembered who they were and whose they were.

Today, we still need that reminder. In a world that measures worth by productivity, Sabbath rest reclaims identity. It says, *"I don't have to earn love—I already have it."* It's a holy rebellion against hurry—a quiet celebration of grace.

If you've been longing for a deeper connection with God, consider this: rest is not just recovery—it's communion. It's a sign that you belong. And it's a place where holiness is not achieved but received.

Prayer:

Lord, thank You for the gift of Sabbath rest. Help me to honor it, not just as a pause, but as a sign of our relationship. Remind me that I am set apart and let my rest reflect Your holiness. Amen.

Journaling Prompt:

What does Sabbath rest mean to you personally? Write about how you might reclaim it as a sacred rhythm and a sign of your belonging to God.

WEEK 40: Rest at the End of the Journey

Scripture:

"As for you, go your way until the end. You will rest, and then at the end of the days you will rise again to receive the inheritance set aside for you."

— *Daniel 12:13 (NLT)*

Reflection:

This verse is God's final word to Daniel—a faithful servant who had seen visions, endured trials, and walked with unwavering devotion. It's not a call to strive, but a call to finish well. To go his way. To rest. To rise.

There's a quiet dignity in this promise. Rest is not just a pause—it's a reward. It's the peace that follows perseverance. And it's paired with resurrection and inheritance—a reminder that our labor in the Lord is never in vain.

For those who walk faithfully, even when the path is unclear, this verse offers deep comfort. God sees. God remembers. And God restores. Rest is not the end—it's the beginning of glory.

If you've been walking a long road, take heart: your journey matters. Your endurance is seen. And your rest is coming—not just in this life, but in the life to come.

Prayer:

Lord, help me to walk faithfully to the end. When I grow weary, remind me of the rest You've promised. Let my life reflect Your hope, and my heart trust in the inheritance You've prepared. Amen.

Journaling Prompt:

What does "going your way until the end" look like in your current season? Write about how God might be inviting you to rest in His promises and persevere with peace.

WEEK 41: Rest Beyond the Reach of Pride

Scripture:

"Wealth is treacherous, and the arrogant are never at rest. They open their mouths as wide as the grave, and like death, they are never satisfied."

— *Habakkuk 2:5a (NLT)*

Reflection:

This verse is a sobering portrait of spiritual unrest. It speaks of arrogance and insatiable desire—of hearts that chase wealth and power but never find peace. Pride, it turns out, is a restless companion. It always wants more. It never settles. It devours joy, leaving the soul hollow.

But God offers a different way—a way of humility, surrender, and trust. Rest doesn't come from accumulation—it comes from alignment. When we let go of the need to prove, possess, or perform, we make space for peace. We stop grasping and start receiving.

This verse invites us to examine our hearts: Are we chasing something that can't satisfy? Are we restless because we've placed our hope in something unstable? The good news is this—Jesus offers rest to the humble. To the weary. To those who come with empty hands and open hearts.

Prayer:

Lord, protect me from the restlessness of pride. Teach me to walk humbly, to trust deeply, and to find satisfaction in You alone. Let my soul be at rest—not because I have much, but because I have You. Amen.

Journaling Prompt:

Is there an area of your life where pride or striving has stolen your rest? Write about how God might be inviting you to release it and receive peace instead.

WEEK 42: Rest Interrupted by Reality

Scripture:

> "Then he came to the disciples and said, 'Go ahead and sleep. Have your rest. But look—the time has come. The Son of Man is betrayed into the hands of sinners.'"
>
> — *Matthew 26:45 (NLT)*

Reflection:

This moment is heavy with sorrow. Jesus, having agonized in prayer, returns to find His disciples asleep—unable to stay awake in His hour of need. His words carry both compassion and urgency: *"Go ahead and sleep... but look—the time has come."*

There's a tension here between rest and readiness. The disciples chose sleep when they were called to watch. And yet, Jesus doesn't scold—He acknowledges the moment. The time has come. The betrayal is unfolding. And rest, for now, must give way to resolve.

This verse reminds us that rest is holy—but timing matters. There are moments when we're called to rise, to pray, to stand. And there are moments when rest must wait. But even then, Jesus speaks gently. He understands our frailty. He meets us in our weakness.

If you've been spiritually drowsy, let this verse awaken you—not with shame, but with grace. The time has come. And Jesus is still inviting you to walk with Him, even if you've just woken up.

Prayer:

Lord, forgive me for the times I've slept through sacred moments. Wake me gently. Strengthen me to stand with You, even when the hour is dark. Let my rest be rooted in readiness, and my heart stay close to Yours. Amen.

Journaling Prompt:

Have you ever missed a moment of spiritual significance because you were weary or distracted? Write about how God might be inviting you to stay awake and walk with Him more attentively.

WEEK 43: Rest Is a Holy Invitation

Scripture:

"Then Jesus said, 'Let's go off by ourselves to a quiet place and rest a while.' He said this because there were so many people coming and going that Jesus and his apostles didn't even have time to eat."

— *Mark 6:31 (NLT)*

Reflection:

Even Jesus needed rest. Even His closest followers, caught in the swirl of ministry and miracles, needed to step away. This verse is not just a moment; it's a model. Jesus didn't push through the exhaustion. He paused. He invited me. He led His friends to a quiet place.

Rest isn't selfish, it's sacred. It's not a retreat from purpose—it's a return to presence. When life is crowded and demands are constant, Jesus whispers, *"Come away."* Not to abandon the mission, but to sustain it.

Notice the tenderness in His words, *"Let's go off by ourselves…"* Rest is relational. It's not just solitude—it's communion. Jesus doesn't send us away to rest—He goes with us. He meets us in the quiet. He restores what's been poured out.

If you've been running empty, hear His invitation today. Step away. Breathe. Eat. Be still. Work can wait. The world will keep spinning. But your soul needs space to be held.

Prayer:

Jesus, thank You for inviting me to rest. Help me to recognize when I need to step away and give me the courage to say yes to Your quiet places. Meet me there and restore my soul. Amen.

Journaling Prompt:

What does your "quiet place" look like right now? Write about how you can make space for rest with Jesus this week, even amid demands.

WEEK 44: Rest in the Revealed Messiah

Scripture:

"Then John testified, 'I saw the Holy Spirit descending like a dove from heaven and resting upon him. I didn't know he was the one, but when God sent me to baptize with water, he told me, "The one on whom you see the Spirit descend and rest is the one who will baptize with the Holy Spirit." I saw this happen to Jesus, so I testify that he is the Chosen One of God.'"

— John 1:32–34 (NLT)

Reflection:

This moment is a revelation. John the Baptist, faithful in his calling, receives confirmation: Jesus is the One. The Spirit descends and *rests* on Him—not briefly, not symbolically, but with divine permanence. It's a sign of identity, authority, and peace.

The Spirit resting on Jesus is more than a visual—it's a declaration. Jesus is the Chosen One. The One who brings not just water, but the Holy Spirit. The One who doesn't just cleanse, but fills. And in that filling, we find rest.

When we recognize Jesus as the One, we stop searching. We stop striving. We rest in the truth of who He is and what He gives. The Spirit that rested on Him now dwells in us. And through Him, we receive peace, power, and presence.

If you've been uncertain or spiritually restless, let this testimony settle your heart: Jesus is the One. The Spirit rests on Him—and through Him, rests on you.

Prayer:

Jesus, You are the Chosen One of God. Thank You for sending Your Spirit to rest on me. Help me to live in that assurance, to stop striving, and to rest in Your presence. Amen.

Journaling Prompt:

Reflect on what it means that the Spirit rested on Jesus and now dwells in you. Write about how that truth brings peace and confidence to your walk with God.

WEEK 45: Rest in God's Comfort

Scripture:

"When we arrived in Macedonia, there was no rest for us. We faced conflict from every direction, with battles on the outside and fear on the inside."

— 2 Corinthians 7:5 (NLT)

Reflection:

Paul's words here are raw and relatable. No rest. Conflict everywhere. Battles outside. Fear within. It's a portrait of spiritual fatigue—of a servant worn thin by the weight of ministry and the pressure of life.

And yet, this verse doesn't end in despair. Just one verse later, Paul writes, *"But God, who encourages those who are discouraged, encouraged us..."* (v.6). That's the rhythm of grace: unrest met by comfort—fear met by presence. Weariness met by divine encouragement.

Rest isn't always the absence of struggle—it's the presence of God in the middle of it. Even when our circumstances are chaotic, His comfort can settle our souls. He doesn't always remove the storm, but He always meets us in it.

If you're facing battles on the outside or fear on the inside, take heart. You're not alone. And rest is still possible—not because the fight is over, but because God is near.

Prayer:

Lord, You see the battles I face and the fears I carry. Meet me in my unrest. Comfort me with Your presence and let Your encouragement bring peace to my soul. Amen.

Journaling Prompt:

Write about a time when you felt unrest both externally and internally. How did God meet you there, and what kind of comfort did He offer?

WEEK 46: Rest in Righteous Justice

Scripture:

"In his justice he will pay back those who persecute you. And God will provide rest for you who are being persecuted and also for us when the Lord Jesus appears from heaven. He will come with his mighty angels, in flaming fire, bringing judgment on those who don't know God and on those who refuse to obey the Good News of our Lord Jesus."

— 2 Thessalonians 1:6–8 (NLT)

Reflection:

This passage is a powerful reminder that rest is not just personal—it's cosmic. It's part of God's justice. For those who suffer, who are persecuted, who endure hardship for the sake of Christ, rest is promised. Not just temporary relief, but eternal restoration.

Paul speaks to a weary church, assuring them that God sees their pain. And more than that—He will act. Justice will come. Wrongs will be made right. And rest will be given. Not earned, not delayed, but delivered when Jesus returns in glory.

This kind of rest is rooted in righteousness. It's not passive, it's purposeful. It's the kind of rest that vindicates, that heals, that honors the faithful. And it reminds us that suffering is not the final word—Jesus is.

If you've felt pressed by trials or misunderstood in your faith, let this verse steady you. Rest is coming. Justice is near. And Jesus will not forget those who have stood firm.

Prayer:

Lord, thank You for Your righteous justice and the promise of rest. Strengthen me when I feel weary or opposed. Help me to trust that You see, You know, and You will restore. Let my hope rest in Your return. Amen.

Journaling Prompt:

Have you ever felt weary from standing firm in your faith? Write about how the promise of God's justice and rest encourages you to keep going.

WEEK 47: Rest Received by Faith

Scripture:

"God's promise of entering his rest still stands, so we ought to tremble with fear that some of you might fail to experience it. For this good news—that God has prepared this rest—has been announced to us just as it was to them. But it did them no good because they didn't share the faith of those who listened to God."

— Hebrews 4:1–2 (NLT)

Reflection:

This passage is both sobering and hopeful. The promise of rest still stands—God has not withdrawn it. But it must be received by faith. The Israelites heard the good news, but it didn't benefit them because they didn't believe it. They missed the rest that was meant for them.

Faith is the doorway to rest. Not effort. Not perfection. Not performance. Just trust. Trust that God is who He says He is. Trust that His rest is real. Trust that His invitation is for *you*.

This kind of rest is more than physical; it's spiritual. It's the profound peace of knowing you're held, loved, and secure. It's the quiet confidence that comes from believing God's Word and walking in it.

If you've been striving or doubting, let this verse call you back to faith. The promise still stands. The rest is still available. And all you need to do is believe.

Prayer:

Lord, thank You that Your promise of rest still stands. Please help me to receive it by faith, not by striving. Strengthen my trust in You and let Your Word settle deep in my heart. Amen.

Journaling Prompt:

Have you ever struggled to believe that God's rest is truly for you? Write about what holds you back, and how you might step into that promise by faith today.

WEEK 48: Rest Still Awaits

Scripture:

"So God's rest is there for people to enter, but those who first heard this good news failed to enter because they disobeyed God."

— *Hebrews 4:6 (NLT)*

Reflection:

This verse is a reminder that rest is not automatic—it's available, but it must be entered. The promise of rest still stands, but disobedience can keep us from experiencing it. The Israelites heard the good news, but they didn't respond with trust or obedience. And so, they wandered.

Rest is more than a pause; it's a posture. It's the soul's response to God's invitation. It's saying yes to His way, even when it's hard. It's choosing to surrender over stubbornness, faith over fear.

This verse also carries hope: *"God's rest is there…"* It hasn't vanished. It hasn't expired. It's still waiting—for you, for me, for all who will listen and obey. If you've missed it before, you haven't missed it forever.

If your heart has been restless, consider this: Is there an area where God is calling you to trust Him more deeply? To obey more fully? Rest begins with that yes.

Prayer:

Lord, thank You that Your rest is still available. Please help me to respond with faith and obedience. Show me where I've resisted and lead me into the peace You've prepared. Amen.

Journaling Prompt:

Is there a place in your life where disobedience or hesitation has kept you from resting? Write about how you might take a step of trust today and enter God's promise.

WEEK 49: Rest Is for Today

Scripture:

"So God set another time for entering his rest, and that time is today. God announced this through David much later in the words already quoted: 'Today when you hear his voice, don't harden your hearts.'"

— *Hebrews 4:7 (NLT)*

Reflection:

This verse is a divine invitation wrapped in urgency: *"Today."* Not tomorrow. Not someday. *Today.* God's rest is not a distant hope—it's a present possibility. And it's offered repeatedly, even after generations of resistance.

The warning is gentle but firm: *"Don't harden your hearts."* Because rest requires response, it's not just hearing God's voice—it's heeding it. It's letting His Word soften what's been calloused by fear, pride, or pain.

This verse reminds us that God is persistent in love. He keeps offering rest. He keeps speaking. And every time we hear His voice, we're given a choice—to open or to resist, to enter or to delay.

If your heart has felt guarded or distant, let this verse be a fresh invitation. Today is the time. Rest is available. And God is speaking.

Prayer:

Lord, thank You for Your persistent invitation to rest. Help me not to harden my heart, but to respond with trust and surrender. Let today be the day I enter more deeply into Your peace. Amen.

Journaling Prompt:

What does "today" mean for you spiritually? Write about how you can respond to God's voice right now and take a step toward deeper rest.

WEEK 50: Rest That Remains

Scripture:

> *"So there is a special rest still waiting for the people of God."*
>
> — *Hebrews 4:9 (NLT)*

Reflection:

This verse is a quiet promise tucked into a powerful chapter. A *special rest*—not ordinary, not fleeting, but sacred and enduring—is still waiting for God's people. It's not lost. It's not locked away. It's waiting.

This rest is more than a day off—it's a divine invitation into God's rhythm. It's the Sabbath-rest of the soul, where striving ceases and communion begins. It's the kind of rest that restores identity, renews strength, and reminds us we belong.

Hebrews 4 speaks of those who missed this rest because of unbelief. But here, the tone shifts: *it still remains.* That means it's not too late. For you, for me, for anyone who hears and believes. God's rest is not a relic—it's a reality.

If you've been longing for deeper peace, let this verse be your reassurance. Rest is not just behind you—it's ahead of you. And it's holy.

Prayer:

Lord, thank You for the special rest that still remains. Help me to receive it with faith, to enter it with joy, and to dwell in it with You. Let my life reflect the peace of Your presence. Amen.

Journaling Prompt:

What does "special rest" mean to you personally? Write about how you can make space for that kind of rest in your daily walk with God.

WEEK 51: Rest from Our Work

Scripture:

"For all who have entered into God's rest have rested from their labors, just as God did after creating the world. So let us do our best to enter that rest. But if we disobey God, as the people of Israel did, we will fall."

— Hebrews 4:10–11 (NLT)

Reflection:

This passage draws a beautiful parallel: just as God rested after creation, we are invited to rest from our striving. Not because the work is unimportant, but because it's complete in Him. Proper rest is not laziness, it's trust. It's the soul's surrender to grace.

The call to "do our best to enter that rest" may seem paradoxical. But it's a reminder that rest takes intention. It's not passive, it's pursued. It requires laying down self-reliance and picking up faith. It means choosing obedience over resistance, and stillness over striving.

This rest is not earned—it's entered. And it's holy. It's the kind of rest that heals, that holds, that humbles. It's the Sabbath of the soul, where we cease from our labor and dwell in God's finished work.

If you've been working hard to prove, perform, or please, let this verse be your invitation: rest is ready. And it's yours to receive.

Prayer:

Lord, thank You for the rest that reflects Your own. Help me to lay down my striving and enter Your grace. Teach me to trust, to obey, and to rest in Your finished work. Amen.

Journaling Prompt:

Where have you been laboring in your own strength? Write about how you can intentionally pursue rest—not as escape, but as sacred surrender.

WEEK 52: Rest That Follows Faithfulness

Scripture:

"And I heard a voice from heaven saying, 'Write this down: Blessed are those who die in the Lord from now on. Yes, says the Spirit, they are blessed indeed, for they will rest from their hard work; for their good deeds follow them!'"

— *Revelation 14:13 (NLT)*

Reflection:

This verse is a heavenly declaration—a voice from above affirming the eternal rest of those who die in the Lord. It's not just comfort, it's a commissioning. *"Write this down,"* the voice says. This truth is too important to forget.

Those who live and die in Christ are *blessed indeed*. Their labor is not lost. Their faithfulness is not forgotten. Their good deeds follow them—not as burdens, but as beautiful echoes of a well-lived life. And now, they rest, not just from toil, but in peace.

This verse reminds us that rest is the reward of righteousness. It's the inheritance of endurance. And it's the Spirit who confirms it—who seals it with divine affirmation. If you've been laboring in love, serving in faith, enduring in hope, take heart: your rest is coming. And it will be holy.

Prayer:

Spirit of God, thank You for the promise of rest for those who die in the Lord. Guide me to live with faith, work with love, and trust my good deeds will endure. Let my life be a testimony of grace. Amen.

Journaling Prompt:

Reflect on what it means to "rest from your hard work" in the Lord. Write about how this promise shapes your view of faithfulness, legacy, and eternity.

FINALLY: There is rest in belonging to the Lord.

Scripture:

"Even if they are not bought back by any of these means, they will still be released in the Year of Jubilee, for the people of Israel belong to me. They are my servants, whom I brought out of the land of Egypt—I am the Lord your God."

— *Leviticus 25:54–55 (NLT)*

Reflection:

These verses are a declaration of divine ownership—not as domination, but as deliverance. God says, *"They belong to me."* Not to debt. Not to circumstance. Not to oppression. To Him. And because of that, they will be released.

This rest is grounded in identity. The Israelites were characterized, not by their servitude, but by their redemption. Their transition from Egypt was facilitated by divine intervention, ensuring they would not remain in bondage. Regardless of external actions, provision for their freedom had already been established.

For us, this is a powerful reminder: we belong to God. Our past does not define us. Our limitations do not imprison us. Our worth is not negotiable. We are His. And because of that, rest is not just possible, it's promised.

If you've felt stuck or unseen, let this truth settle deep: you are God's. You are redeemed. And your release is already written into His story.

Prayer:

Lord, thank You that I belong to You. When I feel bound by fear, failure, or fatigue, remind me of Your redemption. Let me rest in the freedom of being Yours. Amen.

Journaling Prompt:

Write about what it means to you to belong to God. How does that identity shape your sense of rest, freedom, and purpose?

ABOUT THE AUTHOR

Loretta Baker is a Doctor of Ministry in Black Church Leadership, an Elder in the AME Zion church, an ACPE Spiritual Care Professional, and a certified grief care specialist. She is a member of the American Association of Christian Counselors and the Association for Clinical Pastoral Education, Inc.

Rev. Dr. Baker integrates biblical knowledge with an understanding of grief to deliver a relevant message. She offers virtual, multi-media, and in-person instruction through preaching, teaching, and publishing. Her services are designed to help people connect the church and biblical teaching to social issues and collaborate with social service providers to address social concerns.

DrLoretta@Skills4Living-a2z.net

www.Skills4Living-a2z.com

www.ingramcontent.com/pod-product-compliance
Lightning Source LLC
Chambersburg PA
CBHW071157160426
43196CB00011B/2107